Adobe Lightroom CC Keyboard Shortcuts for Windows and Mac OS

By

U. C-Abel Books.

All Rights Reserved

First Edition: 2017

ISBN-13: 978-1543227345
ISBN-10: 1543227341

Published by U. C-Abel Books.

Table of Contents

Acknowledgement.

All thanks to God Almighty for enabling us to bring this work to this point. He is a wonder indeed.

We want to specially appreciate the great company, Adobe Systems for their hard work and style of reasoning in providing the public with helpful programs and resources, and for helping us with some of the tips and keyboard shortcuts included in this book.

Dedication

The dedication of this title goes to users of Adobe Lightroom CC all over the world.

How We Began.

We enjoy using shortcuts because they set us on a high plane that astonishes people around us when we work with them. As wonderful shortcuts users, the worst eyesore we witness in computer operation is to see somebody sluggishly struggling to execute a task through mouse usage when in actual sense shortcuts will help to save that person time. Most people have asked us to help them with a list of keyboard shortcuts that can make them work as smartly as we do and that drove us into research to broaden our knowledge and truly help them as they demanded, that is the reason for the existence of this book. It is a great tool for lovers of shortcuts, and those who want to join the group.

Most times the things we love don't come by easily. It is our love for keyboard shortcuts that made us to bear long sleepless nights like owls just to make sure we get the best out of it, and it is the best we got that we are sharing with you in this book. You cannot be the same at computing after reading this book. The time you entrusted to our care is an expensive possession and we promise not to mess it up.

Thank you.

What to Know Before You Begin.

General Notes.

1.   Most of the keyboard shortcuts you will see in this book refer to the U.S. keyboard layout. Keys for other layouts might not correspond exactly to the keys on a U.S. keyboard. Keyboard shortcuts for laptop computers might also differ.

2.   It is important to note that when using shortcuts to perform any command, you should make sure the target area is active, if not, you may get a wrong result. Example, if you want to highlight all texts you must make sure the text field is active and if an object, make sure the object area is active. The active area is always known by the location where the cursor of your computer blinks.

3.   On a Mac keyboard, the Command key is denoted with the ⌘symbol.

4.   If a function key doesn't work on your Mac as you expect it to, press the Fn key in addition to the function key. If you don't want to press the Fn key every time, you can change your Apple system preferences.

5.   The plus (+) sign that comes in the middle of keyboard shortcuts simply means the keys are

meant to be combined or held down together not to be added as one of the shortcut keys. In a case where plus sign is needed; it will be duplicated (++).

6. Many keyboards assign special functions to function keys, by default. To use the function key for other purposes, you have to press Fn+the function key.

7. For keyboard shortcuts in which you press one key immediately followed by another key, the keys are separated by a comma (,).

8. It is also important to note that the keyboard shortcuts, tips, and techniques listed in this book are for users of Adobe Lihgtroom.

9. To get more information on this title visit ucabelbooks.wordpress.com and search the site using keywords related to it.

10. Our chief website is under construction.

Some Short Forms You Will Find in This Book and Their Full Meaning.

Here are short forms used in this Adobe Lightroom CC Keyboard Shortcuts for Windows and Mac OS book and their full meaning.

1. Win   -   Windows logo key
2. Tab   -   Tabulate Key
3. Shft   -   Shift Key
4. Prt sc   -   Print Screen
5. Num Lock   -   Number Lock Key
6. F   -   Function Key
7. Esc   -   Escape Key
8. Ctrl   -   Control Key
9. Caps Lock   -   Caps Lock Key
10. Alt   -   Alternate Key

CHAPTER 1.

Fundamental Knowledge of Keyboard Shortcuts.

Without the existence of the keyboard, there wouldn't have been anything like keyboard shortcuts so in this chapter we will learn a little about the computer keyboard before moving to keyboard shortcuts.

1. Definition of Computer Keyboard.

This is an input device that is used to send data to computer memory.

Sketch of a Keyboard

1.1 Types of Keyboard.

   i. Standard (Basic) Keyboard.
  ii. Enhanced (Extended) Keyboard.

   i. **Standard Keyboard:** This is a keyboard designed during the 1800s for mechanical typewriters with just 10 function keys (F keys) placed at the left side of it.

  ii. **Enhanced Keyboard:** This is the current 101 to 102-key keyboard that is included in almost all the personal computers (PCs) of nowadays, which has 12 function keys, usually at the top side of it.

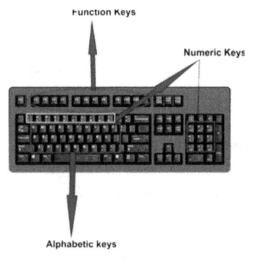

Function Keys

Numeric Keys

Alphabetic keys

1.2 Segments of the keyboard

- Numeric keys.
- Alphabetic keys.
- Punctuation keys.
- Windows Logo key.
- Function keys.
- Special keys.

Numeric Keys: Numeric keys are keys with numbers from **0 - 9**.

Alphabetic Keys: These are keys that have alphabets on them, ranging from **A** to **Z**.

Punctuation Keys: These are keys of the keyboard used for punctuation, examples include comma, full stop, colon, question marks, hyphen, etc.

Windows Logo Key: A key on Microsoft Computer keyboard with its logo displayed on it. Search for this ◼ on your keyboard.

Apple Key: This also known as Command key is a modifier key that you can find on an Apple keyboard. It usually has the image of an apple or command logo on it. Search for this on your Apple keyboard ◼

Function Keys: These are keys that have **F** on them which are usually combined with other keys. They are F1 - F12, and are also in the class called *Special Keys*.

Special Keys: These are keys that perform special functions. They include: Tab, Ctrl, Caps lock, Insert, Prt sc, alt gr, Shift, Home, Num lock, Esc, and many others. Special keys differ according to the type of computer involved. In some keyboard layout, especially laptops, the keys that turn the speaker on/off, the one that increases/decreases volume, the key that turns the computer Wifi on/off are also special keys.

Other Special Keys Worthy of Note.

Enter Key: This is located at the right-hand corner of most keyboards. It is used to send messages to the computer to execute commands, in most cases it is used to mean "Ok" or "Go".

Escape Key (ESC): This is the first key on the upper left of most keyboards. It is used to cancel routines, close menus and select options such as **Save** according to circumstances.

Control Key (CTRL): It is located on the bottom row of the left and right hand side of the keyboard. They also work with the function keys to execute commands using Keyboard shortcuts (key combinations).

Alternate Key (ALT): It is located on the bottom row also of some keyboard, very close to the CTRL key on both side of the keyboard. It enables many editing functions to be accomplished by using some keystroke combinations on the keyboard.

Shift Key: This adds to the roles of function keys. In addition, it enables the use of alternative function of a particular button (key), especially, those with more than one function on a key. E.g. use of capital letters, symbols, and numbers.

1.3. Selecting/Highlighting With Keyboard.

This is a highlighting method or style where data is selected using the computer keyboard instead of a computer mouse.

To do this:

- Move your cursor to the text or object you want to highlight, make sure that area is active,
- Hold down the shift key with one finger,
- Then use another finger to move the arrow key that points to the direction you want to highlight.

1.4 The Operating Modes Of The Keyboard.

Just like the computer mouse, keyboard has two operating modes. The two modes are Text Entering Mode and Command Mode.

a. **Text Entering Mode:** this mode gives the operator/user the opportunity to type text.
b. **Command Mode:** this is used to command the operating system/software/application to execute commands in certain ways.

2. Ways To Improve In Your Typing Skill.

1. Put Your Eyes Off The Keyboard.

This is the aspect of keyboard usage that many don't find funny because they always ask. "How can I put my eyes off the keyboard when I am running away from the occurrence of errors on my file?" My aim is to be fast, is this not going to slow me down?

Of course, there will be errors and at the same time your speed will slow down but the motive behind the introduction to this method is to make you faster than you are. Looking at your keyboard while you type can make you get a sore neck, it is better you learn to touch type because the more you type with your eyes fixed on the screen instead of the keyboard, the faster you become.

An alternative to keeping your eyes off your keyboard is to use the "*Das Keyboard Ultimate*".

2. Errors Challenge You

It is better to fail than to not try at all. Not trying at all is an attribute of the weak and lazybones. When you make mistakes, try again because errors are opportunities for improvement.

3. Good Posture (Position Yourself Well).

Do not adopt an awkward position while typing. You should get everything on your desk organized or arranged before sitting to type. Your posture while typing contributes to your speed and productivity.

4. Practice

Here is the conclusion of everything said above. You have to practice your shortcuts constantly. The practice alone is a way of improvement. "Practice brings improvement". Practice always.

2.1 Software That Will Help You Improve Your Typing Skill.

There are several Software programs for typing that both kids and adults can use for their typing skill. Here is a list of software that can help you improve in your typing: Mavis Beacon, Typing Instructor, Mucky Typing Adventure, Rapid Tying Tutor, Letter Chase Tying Tutor, Alice Touch Typing Tutor and many more. Personally, I love Mavis Beacon.

To learn typing using MAVIS BEACON, install Mavis Beacon software to your computer, start with keyboard lesson, then move to games. Games like **Penguin Crossing, Creature Lab**, or **Space Junk** will help you become a professional in typing. Typing and keyboard shortcuts work hand-in-hand.

Sketch of a computer mouse

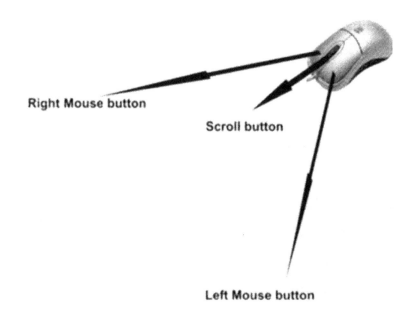

Right Mouse button

Scroll button

Left Mouse button

3. Mouse:

This is an oval-shaped portable input device with three buttons for scrolling, left clicking, and right clicking that enables work to be done effectively on a computer. The plural form of mouse is mice.

3.1 Types of Computer Mouse

- Mechanical Mouse.
- Optical Mechanical Mouse (Optomechanical).
- Laser Mouse.

- Optical Mouse.
- BlueTrack Mouse.

3.2 Forms of Clicking:

Left Clicking: This is the process of clicking the left side button of the mouse. It can also be called *clicking* without the addition of *left*.

Right Clicking: It is the process of clicking the right side button of a computer mouse.

Double Clicking: It is the process of clicking the left side button two times (twice) and immediately.

Triple Clicking: It is the process of clicking the left side button three times (thrice) and immediately.

Double clicking is used to select a word while triple clicking is used to select a sentence or paragraph.

Scroll Button: It is the little key attached to the mouse that looks like a tiny wheel. It takes you up and down a page when moved.

3.3 Mouse Pad: This is a small soft mat that is placed under the mouse to make it have a free movement.

3.4 Laptop Mouse Touchpad

This unlike the mouse we explained above is not external, rather it is inbuilt (comes with the laptop computer). With the presence of a laptop mouse touchpad, an external mouse is not needed to use a laptop, except in a case where it is malfunctioning or the operator prefers to use external one for some reasons.

The laptop mouse touchpad is usually positioned at the end of the keyboard section of a laptop computer. It is rectangular in shape with two buttons positioned below it. The two buttons/keys are used for left and right clicking just like the external mouse. Some laptops come with four mouse keys. Two placed above the mouse for left and right clicking and two other keys placed below it for the same function.

4. Definition Of Keyboard Shortcuts.

Keyboard shortcuts are defined as a series of keys, most times with combination that execute tasks which typically involve the use of mouse or other input devices.

5. Why You Should Use Shortcuts.

1. One may not be able to use a computer mouse easily because of disability or pain.

2. One may not be able to see the mouse pointer as a result of vision impairment, in such case what will the person do? The answer is SHORTCUT.

3. Research has made it known that Extensive mouse usage is related to Repetitive Syndrome Injury (RSI) greatly than the use of keyboard.

4. Keyboard shortcuts speed up computer users, making learning them a worthwhile effort.

5. When performing a job that requires precision, it is wise that you use the keyboard instead of mouse, for instance, if you are dealing with Text Editing, it is better you handle it using keyboard shortcuts than spending more time doing it with your computer mouse alone.

6. Studies calculate that using keyboard shortcuts allows working 10 times faster than working with the mouse. The time you spend looking for the mouse and then getting the cursor to the position you want is lost! Reducing your work duration by 10 times gives you greater results.

5.1 Ways To Become A Lover Of Shortcuts.

1. Always have the urge to learn new shortcut keys associated with the programs you use.
2. Be happy whenever you learn a new shortcut.

3. Try as much as you can to apply the new shortcuts you learnt.
4. Always bear it in mind that learning new shortcuts is worth it.
5. Always remember that the use of keyboard shortcuts keeps people healthy while performing computer activities.

5.2 How To Learn New Shortcut Keys

1. Do a research on them: quick references (a cheat sheet comprehensively compiled like ours) can go a long way to help you improve.
2. Buy applications that show you keyboard shortcuts every time you execute an action with mouse.
3. Disconnect your mouse if you must learn this fast.
4. Read user manuals and help topics (Whether offline or online).

5.3 Your Reward For Knowing Shortcut Keys.

1. You will get faster unimaginably.
2. Your level of efficiency will increase.
3. You will find it easy to use.
4. Opportunities are high that you will become an expert in what you do.
5. You won't have to go for **Office button**, click **New,** click **Blank and Recent**, and click **Create**

just to insert a fresh/blank page. **Ctrl +N** takes care of that in a second.

A Funny Note: Keyboarding and Mousing are in a marital union with Keyboarding being the head, so it will be unfair for anybody to put asunder between them.

5.4 Why We Emphasize On The Use of Shortcuts.

You may never leave your mouse completely unless you are ready to make your brain a box of keyboard shortcuts which will really be frustrating, just imagine yourself learning all shortcuts that go with the programs you use and their various versions. You shouldn't learn keyboard shortcuts that way.

Why we are emphasizing on the use of shortcuts is because mouse usage is becoming unusually common and unhealthy, too. So we just want to make sure both are combined so you can get fast, productive and healthy in your computer activities. All you need to know is just the most important ones associated with the programs you use.

CHAPTER 2.

15 (Fifteen) Special Keyboard Shortcuts.

The fifteen special keyboard shortcuts are fifteen (15) shortcuts every computer user should know.

The following is a list of keyboard shortcuts every computer user should know:

1. **Ctrl + A:** Control A, highlights or selects everything you have in the environment where you are working.

    If you are like **"Wow, the content of this document is large and there is no time to select all of it, besides, it's going to mount pressure on my computer?"** *Using the mouse for this is an outdated method of handling a task like selecting all, Ctrl+A will take care of that in a second.*

2. **Ctrl + C:** Control C copies any highlighted or selected element within the work environment.
    Saves the time and stress which would have been used to right click and click again just to copy. Use ctrl+c.

3. **Ctrl + N:** Control N opens a new window or file.
    Instead of clicking **File, New, blank/ template** *and another* **click,** *just press* **Ctrl + N** *and a fresh page or window will appear instantly.*

4. **Ctrl + O:** Control O opens a new program.
    Use ctrl +O when you want to locate / open a file or program.

5. **Ctrl + P:** Control P prints the active document.
    Always use this to locate the printer dialog box, and thereafter print.

6. **Ctrl + S:** Control S saves a new document or file and changes made by the user.
    Please stop! Don't use the mouse. Just press Ctrl+S and everything will be saved.

7. **Ctrl +V:** Control V pastes copied elements into the active area of the program in use.

Using ctrl+V in a case like this Saves the time and stress of right clicking and clicking again just to paste.

8. **Ctrl + W:** Control W is used to close the page you are working on when you want to leave the work environment.

   "There is a way Debby does this without using the mouse. Oh my God, why didn't I learn it then?" Don't worry, I have the answer. Debby presses Ctrl+W to close active windows.

9. **Ctrl + X:** Control X cuts elements (making the elements to disappear from their original place). The difference between cutting and deleting elements is that in Cutting, what was cut doesn't get lost permanently but prepares itself so that it can be pasted on another location defined by the user.

   *Use ctrl+x when you think **"this shouldn't be here and I can't stand the stress of retyping or redesigning it on the rightful place it belongs"***.

10. **Ctrl + Y:** Control Y undoes already done actions.

    Ctrl+Z brought back what you didn't need? Press Ctrl+ Y to remove it again.

11. **Ctrl + Z:** Control Z redoes actions.

> *Can't find what you typed now or a picture you inserted, it suddenly disappeared or you mistakenly removed it? Press Ctrl+Z to bring it back.*

12. **Alt + F4:** Alternative F4 closes active windows or items.

> *You don't need to move the mouse in order to close an active window, just press **Alt + F4**. Also use it when you are done or you don't want somebody who is coming to see what you are doing.*

13. **Ctrl + F6:** Control F6 Navigates between open windows, making it possible for a user to see what is happening in windows that are active.

> *Are you working in Microsoft Word and want to find out if the other active window where your browser is loading a page is still progressing? Use Ctrl + F6.*

14. **F1:** This displays the help window.

> *Is your computer malfunctioning? Use **F1** to find help when you don't know what next to do.*

15. **F12:** This enables user to make changes to an already saved document.

    F12 is the shortcut to use when you want to change the format in which you saved your existing document, password it, change its name, change the file location or destination, or make other changes to it. It will save you time.

Note: The Control (Ctrl) key on Windows and Linux operating system is the same thing as Command (Cmmd) key on a Macintosh computer. So if you replace Control with Command key on a Mac computer for the special shortcuts listed above, you will get the same result.

CHAPTER 3.

Keyboard Shortcuts for Use in Adobe Lightroom.

About the program: It is an application developed and marketed by Adobe for processing, editing, sharing and organizing photography.

Keyboard Shortcuts in Lightroom.

Use the following list of keyboard shortcuts to enhance your productivity in Adobe Lightroom.

Keys for Working with Panels.

Result	Windows Shortcut	Mac OS Shortcut
Show/hide side panels	Tab	Tab
Show/hide all panels	Shift + Tab	Shift + Tab
Show/hide toolbar	T	T
Show/hide Module Picker	F5	F5

Show/hide Filmstrip	F6	F6
Show/hide left panels	F7	F7
Show/hide right panels	F8	F8
Toggle solo mode	Alt-click a panel	Option-click a panel
Open a new panel without closing soloed panel	Shift-click a panel	Shift-click a panel
Open/close all panels	Ctrl-click a panel	Command-click a panel
Open/close left panels, top to bottom	Ctrl + Shift + 0 - 5	Command + Control + 0 - 5
Open/close right panels, Library and Develop modules, top to bottom	Ctrl + 0 - 9	Command + 0 - 9
Open/close right panels, Slideshow, Print, and Web modules, top to bottom	Ctrl + 1 - 7	Command + 1 - 7

Keys for Navigating Modules.

Result	Windows Shortcut	Mac OS Shortcut

Go to Library module	Ctrl + Alt + 1	Command + Option + 1
Go to Develop module	Ctrl + Alt + 2	Command + Option + 2
Go to Slideshow module	Ctrl + Alt + 3	Command + Option + 3
Go to Print module	Ctrl + Alt + 4	Command + Option + 4
Go to Web module	Ctrl + Alt + 5	Command + Option + 5
Go back / go forward	Ctrl + Alt + Left Arrow / Ctrl + Alt + RIght Arrow	Command + Option + Left Arrow / Command + Option + Right Arrow
Go back to previous module	Ctrl + Alt + Up Arrow	Command + Option + Up Arrow

Keys for Changing Views and Screen Modes.

Result	Windows Shortcut	Mac OS Shortcut
Enter Library Loupe view	E	E

Enter Library Grid view	G	G
Enter Library Compare view	C	C
Enter Library Survey view	N	N
Open selected photo in the Develop module	D	D
Cycle forward / backward through Lights Out modes	L / Shift + L	L / Shift + L
Toggle Lights Dim mode	Ctrl + Shift + L	Command + Shift + L
Cycle screen modes	F	F
Previous screen mode		Shift + F
Switch between Normal and full-screen, hide panels	Ctrl + Shift + F	Command + Shift + F
Go to Normal screen mode	Ctrl + Alt + F	Command + Option + F
Cycle info overlay	I	I
Show/hide info overlay	Ctrl + I	Command + I

Keys for Using a Secondary Window.

Note:

The shortcuts for using the secondary window are the same as the equivalent shortcuts in the Library module, with the Shift key added.

Result	Windows Shortcut	Mac OS Shortcut
Open secondary window	F11	Command + F11
Enter Grid view	Shift + G	Shift + G
Enter normal Loupe view	Shift + E	Shift + E
Enter locked Loupe view	Ctrl + Shift + Enter	Command + Shift + Return
Enter Compare view	Shift + C	Shift + C
Enter Survey view	Shift + N	Shift + N
Enter Slideshow view	Ctrl + Alt + Shift + Enter	Command + Option + Shift + Return
Enter full-screen mode (requires a second monitor)	Shift + F11	Command + Shift + F11
Show/hide Filter bar	Shift + \	Shift + \
Zoom in / zoom out	Ctrl + Shift + = / Ctrl + Shift -	Command + Shift + = / Command + Shift + -

Keys for Managing Photos and Catalogs.

Result	Windows Shortcut	Mac OS Shortcut
Import photos from disk	Ctrl + Shift + I	Command + Shift + I
Open catalog	Ctrl + O	Command +Shift + O
Open Preferences	Ctrl + , (comma)	Command + , (comma)
Open Catalog Settings	Ctrl + Alt + , (comma)	Command + Option + , (comma)
Create new subfolder (segmented tethered capture)	Ctrl + Shift + T	Command +Shift + T
Hide/show tether capture bar	Ctrl + T	Command + T
Create a new folder in the Library module	Ctrl + Shift + N	Command + Shift + N
Create virtual copy (Library and Develop module only)	Ctrl + ' (apostrophe)	Command + ' (apostrophe)
Show in Explorer/Finder (Library and Develop module only)	Ctrl + R	Command + R

Go to next/previous photo in the Filmstrip	Right Arrow/Left Arrow	Right Arrow/Left Arrow
Select multiple folders or collections (in Library, Slideshow, Print, and Web modules)	Shift-click or Ctrl-click	Shift-click or Command-click
Rename photo (in Library module)	F2	F2
Delete selected photo(s)	Backspace or Delete	Delete
Remove selected photo(s) from catalog	Alt + Backspace	Option + Delete
Delete selected photo(s) and move to Recycling Bin (Windows) or Trash (Mac OS)	Ctrl + Alt + Shift + Backspace	Command + Option + Shift + Delete
Delete rejected photo(s)	Ctrl + Backspace	Command + Delete
Edit in Photoshop	Ctrl + E	Command + E
Open in other editor	Ctrl + Alt + E	Command + Option + E
Export selected photo(s)	Ctrl + Shift + E	Command + Shift + E
Export with previous settings	Ctrl + Alt + Shift + E	Command + Option + Shift + E

Open plug-in manager	Ctrl + Alt + Shift + , (comma)	Command + Option + Shift + , (comma)
Print selected photo	Ctrl + P	Command + P
Open Page Setup dialog box	Ctrl + Shift + P	Command + Shift + P

Keys for Comparing Photos in the Library Module.

Result	Windows Shortcut	Mac OS Shortcut
Switch to Loupe view	E or Enter	E or Return
Switch to Grid view	G or Esc	G or Esc
Switch to Compare view	C	C
Switch to Survey view	N	N
Switch from Grid to Loupe view	Spacebar or E	Spacebar or E
Swap select and candidate photos in Compare view	Down Arrow	Down Arrow
Make next photos select and candidate in Compare view	Up Arrow	Up Arrow
Toggle Zoom view	Z	Z
Zoom in / zoom out in Loupe view	Ctrl + = / Ctrl + -	Command + = /

		Command + -
Scroll up/down zoomed photo in Loupe view (also works in Develop and Web modules)	Page Up / Page Down on full-size keyboard	Page Up / Page Down on full-size keyboard
Go to beginning/end of Grid view	Home / End	Home / End
Play impromptu slide show	Ctrl + Enter	Command + Return
Rotate photo right (clockwise)	Ctrl +]	Command +]
Rotate photo left (counterclockwise)	Ctrl + [	Command + [
Increase/decrease Grid thumbnail size	= / -	= / -
Scroll up/down Grid thumbnails	Page Up / Page Down on full-size keyboard	Page Up / Page Down on full-size keyboard
Toggle cell extras	Ctrl + Shift + H	Command + Shift + H
Show/hide badges	Ctrl + Alt + Shift + H	Command + Option + Shift + H
Cycle Grid views	J	J
Open Library view options	Ctrl + J	Command + J
Select multiple discrete photos	Ctrl-click	Command-click

Select multiple contiguous photos	Shift-click	Shift-click
Select all photos	Ctrl + A	Command + A
Deselect all photos	Ctrl + D	Command + D or Command + Shift + A
Select only active photo	Ctrl + Shift + D	Command + Shift + D
Deselect active photo	/	/
Add previous/next photo to selection	Shift + Left/Right Arrow	Shift + Left/Right Arrow
Select flagged photos	Ctrl + Alt + A	Command + Option + A
Deselect unflagged photos	Ctrl + Alt + Shift + D	Command + Option + Shift + D
Group into stack	Ctrl + G	Command + G
Unstack	Ctrl + Shift + G	Command + Shift + G
Toggle stack	S	S
Move to top of stack	Shift + S	Shift + S
Move up in stack	Shift + [	Shift + [
Move down in stack	Shift +]	Shift +]

Keys for Rating and Filtering Photos.

Result	Windows Shortcut	Mac OS Shortcut
Set star rating	1 - 5	1 - 5
Set star rating and go to next photo	Shift + 1 - 5	Shift + 1 - 5
Remove star rating	0	0
Remove star rating and go to next photo	Shift + 0	Shift + 0
Increase/decrease rating by one star	] / [	] / [
Assign a red label	6	6
Assign a yellow label	7	7
Assign a green label	8	8
Assign a blue label	9	9
Assign a color label and go to next photo	Shift + 6 - 9	Shift + 6 - 9
Flag photo as a pick	P	P
Flag photo as a pick and go to next photo	Shift + P	Shift + P
Flag photo as a reject	X	X
Flag photo as a reject and go to next photo	Shift + X	Shift + X
Unflag photo	U	U
Unflag photo and go to next photo	Shift + U	Shift + U
Increase/decrease flag status	Ctrl + Up Arrow / Ctrl + Down Arrow	Command + Up Arrow / Command + Down Arrow
Cycle flag settings	' (back quote)	' (back quote)

Refine photos	Ctrl + Alt + R	Command + Option + R
Show/hide Library Filter bar	\	\
Open multiple filters in the Filter bar	Shift-click filter labels	Shift-click filter labels
Toggle filters on/off	Ctrl + L	Command + L
Find photo in the Library module	Ctrl + F	Command + F

Keys for Working with Collections.

Result	Windows Shortcut	Mac OS Shortcut
Create a new collection in the Library module	Ctrl + N	Command + N
Add to Quick Collection	B	B
Add to Quick Collection and go to next photo	Shift + B	Shift + B
Show Quick Collection	Ctrl + B	Command + B
Save Quick Collection	Ctrl + Alt + B	Command + Option + B
Clear Quick Collection	Ctrl + Shift + B	Command + Shift + B

Set as target collection	Ctrl + Alt + Shift + B	Command + Option + Shift + B

Keys for Working with Metadata and Keywords in the Library Module.

Result	Windows Shortcut	Mac OS Shortcut
Add keywords	Ctrl + K	Command + K
Edit keywords	Ctrl + Shift + K	Command + Shift + K
Set a keyword shortcut	Ctrl + Alt + Shift + K	Command + Option + Shift + K
Add/remove keyword shortcut from selected photo	Shift + K	Shift + K
Enable painting	Ctrl + Alt + K	Command + Option + K
Add a keyword from a keyword set to selected photo	Alt + 1-9	Option + 1-9
Cycle forward / backward through keyword sets	Alt + 0 / Alt + Shift + 0	Option + 0 / Option + Shift + 0

Copy/paste metadata	Ctrl + Alt + Shift + C / Ctrl + Alt + Shift + V	Command + Option + Shift + C / Command + Option + Shift + V
Save metadata to file	Ctrl + S	Command + S
Open Spelling dialog box		Command + :
Check spelling		Command + ;
Open Character palette		Command + Option + T

Keys for Working in the Develop Module.

Result	Windows Shortcut	Mac OS Shortcut
Convert to grayscale	V	V
Auto tone	Ctrl + U	Command + U
Auto white balance	Ctrl + Shift + U	Command + Shift + U
Edit in Photoshop	Ctrl + E	Command + E
Copy/paste Develop settings	Ctrl + Shift + C / Ctrl + Shift + V	Command + Shift + C / Command + Shift + V

Paste settings from previous photo	Ctrl + Alt + V	Command + Option + V
Copy After settings to Before	Ctrl + Alt + Shift + Left Arrow	Command + Option + Shift + Left Arrow
Copy Before settings to After	Ctrl + Alt + Shift + Right Arrow	Command + Option + Shift + Right Arrow
Swap Before and After settings	Ctrl + Alt + Shift + Up Arrow	Command + Option + Shift + Up Arrow
Increase/decrease selected slider in small increments	Up Arrow / Down Arrow or + / -	Up Arrow / Down Arrow or + / -
Increase/decrease selected slider in larger increments	Shift + Up Arrow / Shift + Down Arrow or Shift + + / Shift + -	Shift + Up Arrow / Shift + Down Arrow or Shift + + / Shift + -
Cycle through Basic panel settings (forward/backward)	. (period) / , (comma)	. (period) / , (comma)
Reset a slider	Double-click slider name	Double-click slider name
Reset a group of sliders	Alt-click group name	Option-click group name

Reset all settings	Ctrl + Shift + R	Command + Shift + R
Sync settings	Ctrl + Shift + S	Command + Shift + S
Sync settings bypassing Synchronize Settings dialog box	Ctrl + Alt + S	Command + Option + S
Toggle Auto Sync	Ctrl-click Sync button	Command-click Sync button
Enable Auto Sync	Ctrl + Alt + Shift + A	Command + Option + Shift + A
Match total exposures	Ctrl + Alt + Shift + M	Command + Option + Shift + M
Select White Balance tool (from any module)	W	W
Select the Crop tool (from any module)	R	R
Constrain aspect ratio when Crop tool is selected	A	A
Crop to same aspect ratio as previous crop	Shift + A	Shift + A

Crop from center of photo	Alt-drag	Option-drag
Cycle Crop grid overlay	O	O
Cycle Crop grid overlay orientation	Shift + O	Shift + O
Switch crop between portrait and landscape orientation	X	X
Reset crop	Ctrl + Alt + R	Command + Option + R
Select the Guided Upright tool (also works in the Library module when a photo is selected)	Shift + T	Shift + T
Select the Spot Removal tool	Q	Q
Toggle Brush between Clone and Heal modes when Spot Removal tool is selected	Shift + T	Shift + T
Select the Adjustment	K	K

Brush tool (from any module)		
Select the Graduated Filter tool	M	M
Toggle Mask between Edit and Brush modes when the Graduated Filter or Radial Filter is selected	Shift + T	Shift + T
Increase/decrease brush size	] / [	] / [
Increase/decrease brush feathering	Shift +] / Shift + [	Shift +] / Shift + [
Switch between local adjustment brush A and B	/	/
Temporarily switch from brush A or B to Eraser	Alt-drag	Option-drag
Paint a horizontal or vertical line	Shift-drag	Shift-drag
Increase/decrease Amount	Drag adjustment pin right/left	Drag adjustment pin right/left

Show/hide local adjustment pin	H	H
Show/hide local adjustment mask overlay	O	O
Cycle local adjustment mask overlay colors	Shift + O	Shift + O
Select Targeted Adjustment tool to apply a Tone Curve adjustment	Ctrl + Alt + Shift + T	Command + Option + Shift + T
Select Targeted Adjustment tool to apply a Hue adjustment	Ctrl + Alt + Shift + H	Command + Option + Shift + H
Select Targeted Adjustment tool to apply a Saturation adjustment	Ctrl + Alt + Shift + S	Command + Option + Shift + S
Select Targeted Adjustment tool to apply a Luminance adjustment	Ctrl + Alt + Shift + L	Command + Option + Shift + L
Select Targeted Adjustment tool to apply a	Ctrl + Alt + Shift + G	Command + Option + Shift + G

Grayscale Mix adjustment		
Deselect Targeted Adjustment tool	Ctrl + Alt + Shift + N	Command + Option + Shift + N
Show clipping	J	J
Rotate photo right (clockwise)	Ctrl +]	Command +]
Rotate photo left (counterclockwi se)	Ctrl + [	Command + [
Toggle between Loupe and 1:1 Zoom preview	Spacebar or Z	Spacebar or Z
Zoom in / zoom out	Ctrl + = / Ctrl + -	Command + = / Command + -
Play impromptu slide show	Ctrl + Enter	Command + Return
View Before and After left/right	Y	Y
View Before and After top/bottom	Alt + Y	Option + Y
View Before and After in a split screen	Shift + Y	Shift + Y
View Before only	\	\
Create a new snapshot	Ctrl + N	Command + N
Create a new preset	Ctrl + Shift + N	Command + Shift + N

Create a new preset folder	Ctrl + Alt + N	Command + Option + N
Open Develop view options	Ctrl + J	Command + J

Keys for Working in the Slideshow Module.

Result	Windows Shortcut	Mac OS Shortcut
Play slide show	Enter	Return
Play impromptu slide show	Ctrl + Enter	Command + Return
Pause slide show	Spacebar	Spacebar
Preview slide show	Alt + Enter	Option + Return
End slide show	Esc	Esc
Go to next slide	Right Arrow	Right Arrow
Go to previous slide	Left Arrow	Left Arrow
Rotate photo right (clockwise)	Ctrl +]	Command +]
Rotate photo left (counterclockwise)	Ctrl + [	Command + [
Show/hide guides	Ctrl + Shift + H	Command + Shift + H
Export PDF slide show	Ctrl + J	Command + J
Export JPEG slide show	Ctrl + Shift + J	Command + Shift + J

Export video slide show	Ctrl + Alt + J	Command + Option + J
Create a new slide show template	Ctrl + N	Command + N
Create a new slide show template folder	Ctrl + Shift + N	Command + Shift + N
Save slide show settings	Ctrl + S	Command + S

Keys for Working in the Print Module.

Result	Windows Shortcut	Mac OS Shortcut
Print	Ctrl + P	Command + P
Print one copy	Ctrl + Alt + P	Command + Option + P
Open Page Setup dialog box	Ctrl + Shift + P	Command + Shift + P
Open Print Settings dialog box	Ctrl + Alt + Shift + P	Command + Option + Shift + P
Go to first page	Ctrl + Shift + Left Arrow	Command + Shift + Left Arrow
Go to last page	Ctrl + Shift + Right Arrow	Command + Shift + Right Arrow
Go to previous page	Ctrl + Left Arrow	Command + Left Arrow

Go to next page	Ctrl + Right Arrow	Command + Right Arrow
Show/hide guides	Ctrl + Shift + H	Command + Shift + H
Show/hide rulers	Ctrl + R	Command + R
Show/hide page bleed	Ctrl + Shift + J	Command + Shift + J
Show/hide margins and gutters	Ctrl + Shift + M	Command + Shift + M
Show/hide image cells	Ctrl + Shift + K	Command + Shift + K
Show/hide dimensions	Ctrl + Shift + U	Command + Shift + U
Play impromptu slide show	Ctrl + Enter	Command + Return
Rotate photo right (clockwise)	Ctrl +]	Command +]
Rotate photo left (counterclockwise)	Ctrl + [	Command + [
Create a new print template	Ctrl + N	Command + N
Create a new print template folder	Ctrl + Shift + N	Command + Shift + N
Save print settings	Ctrl + S	Command + S

Keys for working in the Web Module.

Result	Windows Shortcut	Mac OS Shortcut
Reload web gallery	Ctrl + R	Command + R
Preview in browser	Ctrl + Alt + P	Command + Option + P
Play impromptu slide show	Ctrl + Enter	Command + Return
Export web gallery	Ctrl + J	Command + J
Create a new web gallery template	Ctrl + N	Command + N
Create a new web gallery template folder	Ctrl + Shift + N	Command + Shift + N
Save web gallery settings	Ctrl + S	Command + S

Keys for Using Help.

Result	Windows Shortcut	Mac OS Shortcut
Display current module shortcuts	Ctrl + /	Command + /
Hide current module shortcuts	Click	Click
Go to current module Help	Ctrl + Alt + /	Command + Option + Shift + /
Open Community Help	F1	F1

Customer's Page.

This page is for customers who enjoyed Adobe Lightroom CC Keyboard Shortcuts for Windows and Mac.

Our beloved and respectable reader, we thank you very much for your patronage. Please we will appreciate it more if you rate and review this book; that is if it was helpful to you. Thank you.

Download Our EBooks Today For Free.

In order to appreciate our customers, we have made some of our titles available at 0.00. They are totally free. Feel free to get a copy of the free titles.

Here are books we give to our customers free of charge:

(A) For Keyboard Shortcuts in Windows check:

Windows 7 Keyboard Shortcuts.

(B) For Keyboard Shortcuts in Office 2016 for Windows check:

Word 2016 Keyboard Shortcuts For Windows.

(C) For Keyboard Shortcuts in Office 2016 for Mac check:

<u>OneNote 2016</u> Keyboard Shortcuts For Macintosh.

Follow <u>this link</u> to download any of the titles listed above for free.

Note: Feel free to download them from our website or your favorite bookstore today. Thank you.

Other Books By This Publisher.

Titles for single programs under Shortcut Matters Series are not part of this list.

S/N	Title	Series
Series A: Limits Breaking Quotes.		
1	Discover Your Key Christian Quotes	Limits Breaking Quotes
Series B: Shortcut Matters.		
1	Windows 7 Shortcuts	Shortcut Matters
2	Windows 7 Shortcuts & Tips	Shortcut Matters
3	Windows 8.1 Shortcuts	Shortcut Matters
4	Windows 10 Shortcut Keys	Shortcut Matters
5	Microsoft Office 2007 Keyboard Shortcuts For Windows.	Shortcut Matters
6	Microsoft Office 2010 Shortcuts For Windows.	Shortcut Matters
7	Microsoft Office 2013 Shortcuts For Windows.	Shortcut Matters
8	Microsoft Office 2016 Shortcuts For Windows.	Shortcut Matters
9	Microsoft Office 2016 Keyboard Shortcuts For Macintosh.	Shortcut Matters
10	Top 11 Adobe Programs Keyboard Shortcuts	Shortcut Matters
11	Top 10 Email Service Providers Keyboard Shortcuts	Shortcut Matters
12	Hot Corel Programs Keyboard Shortcuts	Shortcut Matters

13	Top 10 Browsers Keyboard Shortcuts	Shortcut Matters
14	Microsoft Browsers Keyboard Shortcuts.	Shortcut Matters
15	Popular Email Service Providers Keyboard Shortcuts	Shortcut Matters
16	Professional Video Editing with Keyboard Shortcuts.	Shortcut Matters
17	Popular Web Browsers Keyboard Shortcuts.	Shortcut Matters

Series C: Teach Yourself.

1	Teach Yourself Computer Fundamentals	Teach Yourself
2	Teach Yourself Computer Fundamentals Workbook	Teach Yourself

Series D: For Painless Publishing

1	Self-Publish it with CreateSpace.	For Painless Publishing
2	Where is my money? Now solved for Kindle and CreateSpace	For Painless Publishing
3	Describe it on Amazon	For Painless Publishing